The Prestige S

London Trans

John Banks

Photography by G H F Atkins

Cover: The distinctive Metro-Scania made its mark in London as in many other parts of the country. Its mismatched front windscreens and phenomenal acceleration in traffic set it apart in both looks and performance from its contemporaries. Here, at King's Cross, one of London Transport's examples contrasts with the better-known Routemaster in September 1978.

Title page: An early thirties cameo of an LGOC LT-class double-decker with Chiswick's second style of enclosed-staircase body in original condition. **LT684** (**GT5092**), in a lively traffic scene in Whitehall, was on route 11A passing the Cenotaph in January, 1932. Other buses are mostly members of the NS class, some with solid tyres. LT684 had entered service in September 1931 and was just over three months old. It lasted until June 1949.

Opposite page: Few sightings were more rare in London in 1935 than that of a Q-type double-decker. There were only ever five of them in the LPTB fleet, three of which never worked in the Central Area. Q2 and Q3 did for a time, before being sent to join Q4, Q5 and Q188 in the Country Area. **Q3** (**AYV616**), working the 52 from Middle Row (North Kensington) garage, was photographed at Victoria in August 1935.

Rear cover: More than one Northerner journeying south on the old A1 in the 1950s measured his approach to London by marking the first sighting of a green double-decker and then the first red one. In those days they were always RTs, of course, and here Geoffrey Atkins has put one of each onto a fine view taken at a rally in Nottingham.

Below: After Victoria, Golders Green bus station was perhaps Geoffrey Atkins's most often-visited location in London. In this September 1954 view examples of the RT and RF families of standard vehicles are on routes 2, 28, 83, 210 and 240.

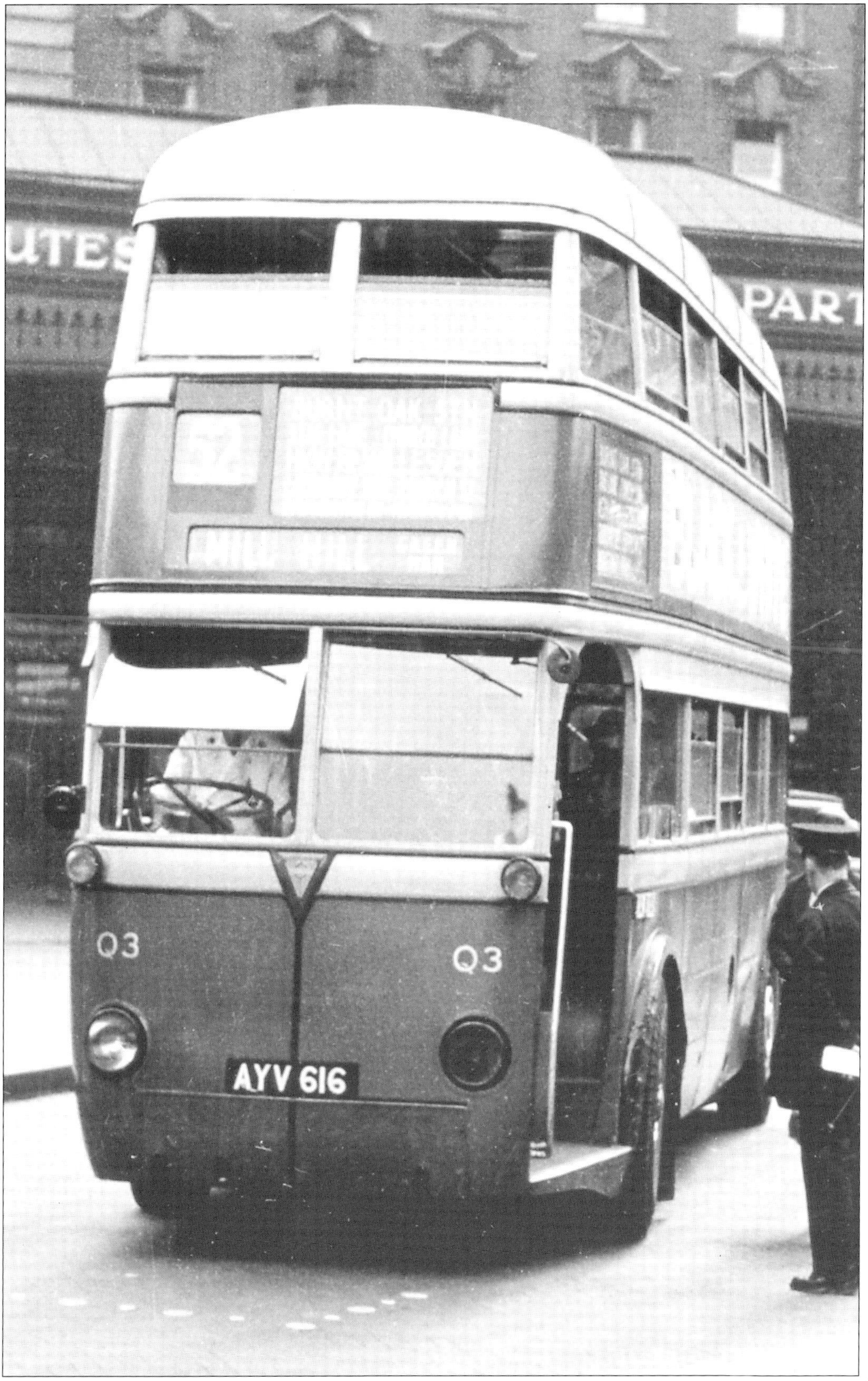
UTES
PART
Q3
Q3
AYV 616

INTRODUCTION

A view of the London General Omnibus Company's LT50, an open-staircase, six-wheeled double-decker, is the first photograph of a London bus that the writer can recall seeing. It was a beautifully produced, creamy-sepia illustration in a magazine when I was very young in the late 1940s. I was profoundly impressed: I had not seen buses with six wheels before, and the photograph was captioned as being of "a modern London bus". The magazine must have been rather old, no doubt one which my parents had had for some years, perhaps purchased before the war. I recall thinking it strange that modern buses in London should be so very different from those in the provinces (in other words, Kingston-upon-Hull, where I lived and outside whose borders I knew little or nothing of the bus scene) in the 1940s.

The principal differences, of course, were the outside staircase and the three-axled chassis.

Both had featured on prewar Hull Corporation buses, but such vehicles had long gone to the scrapyard by the time a certain small boy was sitting up and taking notice. In fact, LT50 was withdrawn in August 1948, which would be about the time I saw the magazine illustration. It was not so very "modern", after all, but the impression was made, from which grew a lifelong fascination with public transport in the Capital.

I was unable to do anything about that interest then; indeed, did not know how to do anything. But when I eventually went to live and work in London in 1961 and found various sources of information and illustrations (the Ian Allan bookshop at Hampton Court, that other amazing bookshop Lens of Sutton, the London Transport photographic library at 55 Broadway, contact with such stalwarts of the collecting and photography world as D W K Jones, J F Higham and G J Robbins) the enthusiasm was allowed to flower and has done for nearly four decades since.

Before that 1961 move, I had visited the Capital only three times. The first, in about 1956, was with parents and sister in the old family Ford 8. The itinerary precluded much bus spotting but I recall being struck dumb with the hundreds of RTs and RTLs that I saw. I knew the difference, but didn't know enough to spot the RTW as being different again. The fact that the AECs and Leylands were identical apart from the radiator and engine sound was another source of wonder. To this day I remain convinced that I saw an STL at London Bridge station on that trip, but have been earnestly assured that I could not have, as they had all been withdrawn by then. Thirty previously withdrawn STLs were sold in 1956, perhaps it was one of them on some non-PSV duty. Whatever it was, it wasn't an RT, because I remarked that it didn't have the faired-in front-nearside mudguard so evident on the London fleet and which was quite new to me. Many years later I realised that the RLHs didn't have the distinctive RT-type mudguard, but did they ever run to London Bridge?

My second trip was for the 1960 Commercial Motor Show, for by then I had a job in the office of a bulk liquids haulage company, was widening my interests and managed to obtain grudging assent for a day off. Overnight train journeys with a day at the show sandwiched between left little energy for anything else, but the Routemaster on the AEC stand gave a sign of things to come. (I didn't know then that the first Routemaster had been on the streets since 1956.)

The third visit was for the job interview. I got the job, moved down, settled in, and began to learn and love London Transport. Many an afternoon was spent sitting in the downstairs front-nearside seat of an RT or RTL, watching the driver. "As far as you're going," was always my response when the conductor came for my fare. Thus did I discover many parts of London that would have otherwise been quite unknown to me. Such was my interest in the operation as viewed from that front seat that I vowed that one day I would drive London buses. I did, too, eventually: RTs and RMs from Hendon, RMs and RMLs from Chalk Farm - but that's another story.

I soon bought a camera, but had no success whatever with my pictures. Someone who did, however, and who had been doing so since 1927, was the Nottingham-based transport photographer Geoffrey Atkins, whose visits to London, cameras at the ready, began in the 1920s. Geoffrey still takes photographs in his home town of Nottingham and so is one of the few, perhaps the only, transport photographer to have taken pictures in each of nine consecutive decades.

To look through the Atkins London collection is to be taken on a guided tour of all that was best in standard London designs from the drawing office at Chiswick. Geoffrey, always having had an appreciation of bus and coach bodywork as his first interest, concentrated on the standard types to the almost total exclusion of vehicles acquired by the London Passenger Transport Board from independent operators. Although he can recall seeing ex-independent Leyland Titans, particularly at Victoria, in the 1930s, he found them of less interest. On the other hand, the postwar Leyland-bodied Titan PD1s of the STD class *were* of interest but somehow always seemed to evade Geoffrey's lens. Whilst regretting the absences, it is as well that we recall that Geoffrey's photography was pursued as a personal interest. Publication was never a goal and, indeed, many of the pictures never have been published. Not all of them can appear in this book, and the task of deciding what to leave out has been, as ever, an onerous one.

The photographer's visits to London usually took the form of "half-day" excursions by train from Nottingham. An arrival at Marylebone station was followed by an instructive few hours in the Capital during which there was always time for some bus photography. Victoria bus terminal, on the forecourt of the railway station, and the coach station a few hundred yards away were often visited in both prewar and postwar periods. In later years, Golders Green became a favourite haunt. There were often purposeful rides out to certain locations for a specific type of new bus, for example Hendon in 1937 for the magnificent portraits of the STD-class Leyland Titan TD4s, which were running out of Hendon garage.

The London General Omnibus Company Limited (usually abbreviated to LGOC or General) was founded in 1856. On 1st July 1933 it formed the core of a new body with monopoly powers to provide bus, trolleybus, tram and railway services in greater London, the London Passenger Transport Board (LPTB). On 1st January 1948 the LPTB disappeared and in its place arose the London Transport Executive (LTE). The LTE was part of the nationalised

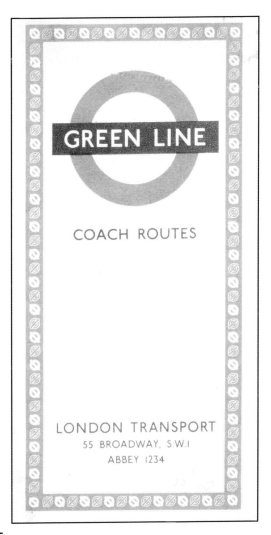

5

transport concern known as the British Transport Commission (BTC) and it oversaw the management of London Transport until the last day of December 1962. On 1st January 1963 London's passenger transport services came under the control of the London Transport Board (LTB), directly responsible to the Minister of Transport. This arrangement lasted a mere seven years, for on 1st January 1970 there was yet another change, and a disastrous one, when management of London Transport was handed to the Greater London Council who promptly gave away the Country Area fleet and routes, including Green Line, to the National Bus Company.

The development of the London motor bus forms a continuous thread from the turn of the century up to the late-1950s, regardless of which body actually owned the organisation. The LGOC was not alone on London's streets, either before or after the 1914 - 1918 war, and had to contend with much competition from independent operators, to which it disparagingly referred as "pirates". Some were, and deserved the appellation, but others were not and provided vehicles and services which in some cases exceeded those of the General in quality.

The very first motor bus on London's streets appeared in 1899. Thus the mechanical conveyance of passengers in the Capital just manages to be a 19th Century phenomenon. The LGOC and several other operators experimented for five or six years with an amazing array of motor buses, some relatively successful, others downright disasters. Two large concerns, Vanguard and Union Jack, were absorbed by the LGOC on 1st July 1908, thus bringing to an end a period of somewhat cut-throat competition and giving the General a fleet of 899 motor buses. Other well-established operators, Thomas Tilling and Birch Brothers for example, continued independently until swallowed up into the LPTB in the early 1930s.

One of the most important results of the Vanguard merger was that that concern's vehicle building works at Walthamstow was a little while later separated from the parent firm and set up as the Associated Equipment Company Limited. Thus the legendary AEC was born. AEC remained the major supplier of London buses until the 1960s.

Back in 1908, however, the search was on for a reliable standard bus chassis. An engineer by the name of Frank Searle joined the LGOC in 1907 and within three months was Chief Engineer. He it was who scotched a plan to standardise on the Wolseley bus chassis. Searle recommended that the Company build its own buses at Walthamstow. The first production was the X type, the first of which was licensed in December 1909. Three hundred were ordered, but only 61 were built and little of the X's design went into the next Walthamstow model. This was the Searle masterpiece, the B type, of which well over 2,500 examples were built, although bonnet numbers into the upper six-thousands were used.

The B type was immensely successful and put the LGOC on a sound footing, enabling it to sweep quickly away its remaining horse buses. Vehicle design matters did not stand still, however, and the B type was soon rather dated. After the First World War it was still in production, but in 1919 the new K type appeared. This had the driver alongside the engine, in the so-called forward-control position. The new bus had room for 44, sometimes 46, passengers, and by 1926 1,132 had been built, including some single-deckers. 1920 saw the last of the X types withdrawn and the first of the S type introduced. This looked much like the K, but was a 54-seater, and 969 of them in several versions were built between 1920 and 1927.

In August 1922 the General was outraged at the appearance of a Leyland double-decker on its prestige route 11 to Liverpool Street station. This was the first of the postwar independents, running under the fleetname "EXPRESS". There were to be many others, the best of which stayed the course. It took an Act of Parliament to get rid of them.

The better independents put vehicles onto the streets of London which made the General's fleet look distinctly second-rate. Something had to be done. The Leylands and Dennises were matched by the London General NS type, which made its debut in 1923. The NS was a more powerful bus than the S, with a lower centre of gravity and thus a lower boarding platform, and had 52 seats. As originally designed it had solid tyres, no roof, and an open driving cab. Over the next decade most examples were fitted with covered tops, pneumatic tyres and enclosed cabs. The NS class eventually totalled 2,394 units, and the last ran in passenger service in 1937, although some survived the Second World War after conversion to service vehicles.

The independents more or less laughed at the NS. In 1927 alarm bells were once again triggered in the LGOC boardroom when rumours began to circulate of a plan by the

London Public Omnibus Company to put a fleet of six-wheeled double-deckers into service. Both Guy and Karrier were apparently involved in these discussions, but the former got the order and on 9th September 1927 the first of fourteen 60-seat, three-axle Guys entered service on route 529 with the "PUBLIC" fleetname emblazoned across their smart navy-blue body panels. Public attracted many of the smaller independents into merging with it; they saw a protective umbrella under which to continue the fight against the General. Public eventually sold out to the General, an act regarded as a betrayal by many of its consituents.

In the meantime, however, the LGOC was determined to steal the Public's thunder, and hastily commissioned a six-wheeled chassis from the Associated Daimler Company (a temporary and unsuccessful joining of forces by AEC and Daimler). The result was a twelve-strong class of ADC Type 802 three-axle vehicles which became the LS class. "LS" stood for "London Six", and the bonnet number was proudly displayed with that legend underneath it. They were not much to be proud of, unfortunately. Although the first did beat the Public's Guy into service by a short head, the General had trouble with the licensing authorities over them. Some originally had enclosed platforms and staircases, but official opposition to this feature led to all of them being standardised as open-platform 60-seaters, as opposed to anything from the 66 to 72 seats which could be fitted into the enclosed-staircase version.

By this time the LGOC's engineering and coachbuilding activities had become well-established at Chiswick Works, and there a plan to shorten an LS and fit it with a new body was mooted. The body was actually built in 1929, but never went onto an LS. Instead it was fitted to the first AEC Renown as LT1. Another Chiswick plan was to build its own buses complete: chassis, bodies and even engines. Seven appeared, four double-deckers and three single-deckers, before the scheme was quietly forgotten in the face of the enormous success of three new productions from the AEC factory.

An engineer of great renown, J G Rackham, had been enticed away from Leyland Motors, for whom he had designed the Titan, by AEC, and he got to work at once to produce the AEC Renown, Regent and Regal models. Here at last was worthy competition for the Leyland Titans of the independents, and the General went for them in a big way. There were eventually 1,429

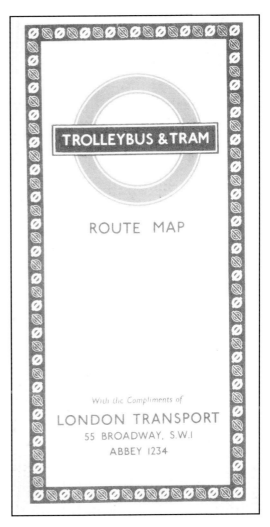

TROLLEYBUS & TRAM

ROUTE MAP

With the Compliments of

LONDON TRANSPORT
55 BROADWAY, S.W.1
ABBEY 1234

six-wheeled AEC Renowns, 1,139 of the original short-wheelbase AEC Regents and 798 single-deck AEC Regals: respectively the LT, ST and T classes. The four-wheeled version of the double-decker became the standard for the future, and a long-wheelbase version proliferated to the tune of 2,701 examples as the STL class.

In the 1920s the LGOC had working agreements with several other operators: in the Central Area Thomas Tilling was the most notable. In the Country Area East Surrey and National, at Reigate in the south and Watford in the north, were the cooperating concerns. In 1929 the LGOC started running express coach services to compete with much independent activity in this field, and this modest start was the birth of Green Line Coaches Limited. In 1932, Green Line as well as the Reigate and Watford operations were reorganised as London General Country Services Limited, which in turn became the Country Department of the LPTB on 1st July 1933.

The LPTB acquired the entire LGOC, Green Line and LGCS fleets and simply carried on where the General had left off so far as vehicle policy was concerned. The LPTB acquired-vehicle total was eventually 6,732, rather more than had been in the fleets of the LGOC and its subsidiaries. The balance of several hundreds came from the independents who were compulsorily taken over by that Act of Parliament previously mentioned as having been necessary to get rid of them. There were some 35 makes of chassis, and the bodies thereon ranged in shape and size from small village buses with 12 seats to maximum capacity double-deckers for inner-city use.

Leaving aside AEC and ADC, upon which the LGOC had been - and therefore the new LPTB would be - standardised, chassis makes ran alphabetically from AJS to W & G. The most numerous were Leyland, with 295 examples, Dennis (231) and Gilford (220). Tilling-Stevens managed 98 units but no other reached 50, and many were in single figures. Some, indeed, such as Minerva, BAT, Sunbeam and Brockway contributed only one each.

The LPTB set about sorting this lot out, and many of the ex-independent buses and coaches were put into store and sold without further use. The best of them, usually the Leylands, Dennises and Gilfords, survived into the late 1930s; the last Leyland Titan, for example, was withdrawn in 1939. The AECs and ADCs fared a little better, slotting as they did into established standard classes of similar chassis. Thus the last true ex-independent bus (STL553, which had come from the rather aptly named Charles Pickup) was not withdrawn from passenger service until February 1950.

The STL and T classes were developed, but the tradition of using smaller non-standard types for special purposes was continued. The LGOC had had three Dennis Hs and 25 Dennis Lances, as well as the three fascinating ST-bodied Daimler CH6s in its double-deck fleet; whilst single-deckers of non-AEC origin included a Bean and a fleet of Dennis Darts. The new Board did not hesitate to go elsewhere for its buses if there was no AEC product to fill a particular need: hence the large fleet of Leyland Cubs in three versions. That does not explain the Leyland TD4 Titans of the STD-class in 1937, however. Fine buses that they were, they did nothing of which contemporary STLs were incapable.

The 1939 - 1945 war brought utility buses on Leyland Titan, Guy Arab, Daimler and Bristol chassis into the fleet, and immediately after the war some Leyland PD1 Titans and PS1 Tigers were bought. The postwar years, however, are notable for the development of the RT, first seen in 1938, and the Routemaster. Across the whole range of variants, the postwar RT and the Routemaster accounted for nearly ten thousand buses entering the London Transport fleet between 1947 and 1968.

The whole glorious story culminated in the magnificent FRM. This rear-engined, front-entrance version of the Routemaster was the final flowering of the standards of excellence inaugurated by Searle of the LGOC back in 1907 and continued under his successors, notably Albert Stanley (later Lord Ashfield) and Frank Pick, at Chiswick through the twenties, thirties and forties. The most saddening aspect of the death of this fine tradition is that the FRM, and therefore any hope of continuing specific London Transport bus development, was killed off by political interference on the part of people who knew not the slightest thing about providing vital and essential passenger services in a capital city.

The best of that tradition and the first shadows of the new era are covered in this album of Geoffrey Atkins photographs. Readers are reminded that the book makes no claim to be either a comprehensive history or a fleet list.

John Banks
Romiley, Cheshire
June 2000

8

Bridges and Buses

Above: Westminster Bridge circa 1931, in the very early days of Green Line operations, has **T207** (**GK5493**) followed by **T226** (**GN2018**). T207 was the first of the batch of 100 ordered when Green Line took the decision to switch to front-entrance 30-seaters. It was heading through on route K from Caterham to Hemel Hempstead. T223 was terminating in London. Both had Duple bodies, though others in the batch carried Ransomes or Weymann coachwork.

Below: In July 1952 a fine view of Tower Bridge chanced to include **RT2279** (**KGU308**) crossing on route 78 to Shoreditch Church.

LGOC Types at Victoria

Above: The unfortunate London Sixes spent some time on route 16 out of Cricklewood garage in the nineteen-thirties. In this August 1935 view, **LS11** (**YW7988**), surrounded by new STLs as well as Chiswick's ST and LT classes, was beginning to look very dated.

Below: By comparison with the rare and elusive LS vehicles, the NS class was to be seen all over the network. This splendid picture is of **NS964** (**XP6663**) in August 1936, its conductor in conference with the driver. The NS was also on the 16 and was in exactly the same spot as LS11 had been a year earlier.

Traffic Scenes at Victoria

Above: Four distinctive RT family variants in May 1955. Cravens-bodied **RT1512 (KGK771)** on the left is waiting to leave on route 38A for Loughton Station. In the foreground are normal and roof-box versions of the standard RT: **RT4580 (NLP573)** and **RT201 (HLW188)** represent late and early examples of the type. On the right is **RTL1467 (NLE752)** on the 25 for Becontree Heath.

Page 12: This August 1930 scene is redolent of the London General era. Solid-tyred NSs with roofs are in the majority, but **K118 (LU8337)** is on the 38A and another London Six, **LS10 (YW7986)**, waits to head north up the Edgware Road on the 16A. The inspectors' control tower allows the eye of authority to attempt to keep track of what is going on.

Page 13: Four years later the NSs have pneumatic tyres and the K class has disappeared, although the control tower is still there. The six-wheeled LT is well to the fore with early and late examples of the class present. In this September 1934 scene are open-staircase **LT95 (GH3842)**, **NS1674 (XW9822)**, another NS which cannot be identified and Bluebird **LT1307 (GX5253)**.

Page 14: By August 1950 the control tower had gone and the buses were all of the RT family in this quite remarkable shot of a torrential London downpour. Pedestrians are, perhaps understandably, conspicuous by their absence, although one intrepid gent under an umbrella can be spotted sprinting for his bus.

Page 15: The early postwar condition of the RT family is well shown in this view, another from August 1950. The reduced blind displays and cream upper-deck window surrounds are evident. Strangely, blind provision was increased and use of cream paint much reduced as things improved in the early 1950s. The buses were **RT414 (HLX231)**, **SRT55 (FXT76)** and **RT3079 (KXW188)**. The hybrid SRT, constructed from a refurbished prewar STL chassis and a new RT body, was on the 16 from Cricklewood. The SRTs were heartily disliked by platform staff, as were the borrowed Tilling Bristols and as had been the LSs on the same route. Longer-serving Cricklewood crews would have worked all three and could perhaps justifiably have bemoaned such a series of very unpopular allocations.

The ST Class at Victoria

These two September 1934 views show ordinary members of the ST-class working route 76 from Tottenham garage. There is nothing special about the buses. They would not have caused even the most dedicated contemporary enthusiast to cross the street for a closer look but how valuable such pictures are to us today. They depict the Chiswick-inspired condition in which the class ran between 1934/1935 and 1939 when war broke out and standards inevitably began to decline. From the attitudes of its driver and conductor, **ST29** (**GH603**) seems to be reversing, whilst the absent crew of **ST690** (**GN4786**) are no doubt in the canteen enjoying a well-earned tea break before taking their bus back to Edmonton, Park Road.

The LT-Class at Victoria

A pair of September 1934 views produced an example each of the first and second of the three styles of bodywork originally fitted to vehicles in the range LT151 to LT950. **LT740** (**GT5165**), coasting in to the route 38 stand *(above)*, has the earlier style. **LT511** (**GP3418**), standing at the back of the queue of vehicles serving the 25 group of routes, has the correct style of body for its bonnet number. In neither case would the body have been that fitted when the vehicles were new. The background of the LT511 view contains much of interest: behind the bus is the small, brick-built staff canteen for Victoria bus station and in the top right-hand corner of the picture an enterprising restaurant was offering high tea for two shillings and "theatre dinner" for four (10p and 20p).

The STL-class at Victoria

Very much the same might be said for these two photographs as was included in the caption on page 16, except that we have moved on three years, to August and September 1937, and the 76 is now host to standard members of the STL-class. **STL804** (**BXD463**) had been left with both windscreen and ventilator open *(above)*, so doubtless it was a warm day. The picture of **STL877** (**CGJ37**) tells a story. It looks as if the driver is just applying his handbrake after coming to rest, but the conductor is not visible. The odds are that he had jumped off the platform a few yards back and nipped into the canteen to order the cups of tea. Perhaps the elegant young couple approaching the camera had just feasted on the two-shilling high tea.

STLs at Victoria

Above: The Tottenham garage STs, running as AR23 and AR3, *(see page 16)* and **STL257 (AUC548)** of the second Chiswick design, with running number AR15, were possibly three consecutive timings on route 76 on that day in September 1934. STL257 was one of the first to appear after the formation of the LPTB. It had entered service in January 1934 and illustrates the continued use of G^{ENERA}L fleetname transfers in the period before the L^{ONDON TRANSPOR}T style was introduced in June 1934. *Below:* Among garages to receive new STLs in place of NSs in 1937 (the last year of the NS in passenger service) was Cricklewood, whose **STL2074 (DLU73)** was on route 92 from Sudbury Town Station in September 1937. The change from NS to STL operation had taken place the previous May.

STLs on the 52

STL173 (AGX504) *(above)* was of the first type of STL, designed by the LGOC. The design's uncompromisingly upright front allowed seating for 60 on a two-axle chassis for the first time. It was on the 52 in May 1937. It was rather surprisingly a Camberwell garage allocation, which must have involved a lot of dead mileage. Middle Row's **Q3 (AYV616)**, seen behind the STL, was at that time a regular performer on the 52. **STL2208 (CYT711)**, also on the 52 in 1937, was one of a batch which was allocated a miscellany of London registration number oddments in various series not otherwise used on London buses. The uncertainty as to how the three-piece destination display should be arranged was already evident in the 1930s and was not finally resolved until the later RTs and the Routemaster saw the final abandonment of the roof route number box.

Bluebird LTs

The magnificent Bluebird LTs in the tragically short heyday of the London Passenger Transport Board before the outbreak of war are seen in these mid 1930s traffic scenes of **LT1342** (**GX5286**) on the 48D to Golders Green *(above)* and **LT1228** (**GW5913**) in stately procession across Trafalgar Square with the National Gallery in the background. The 1931 Bluebird LT - so called because of its blue upholstery - was almost the final flowering of the LGOC's design development which stretched back in an unbroken line to Frank Searle's X type of 1909. It could also be seen in the first STL, which was also the penultimate purely LGOC-designed double-decker *(see page 20)* and the very last, the "leaning-back" STL *(see page 19)*. Through the mid and late 1930s, under the LGOC's successor, the LPTB, the Chiswick double-decker assumed the more rounded, streamlined profile as seen on later STLs and the first RTs.

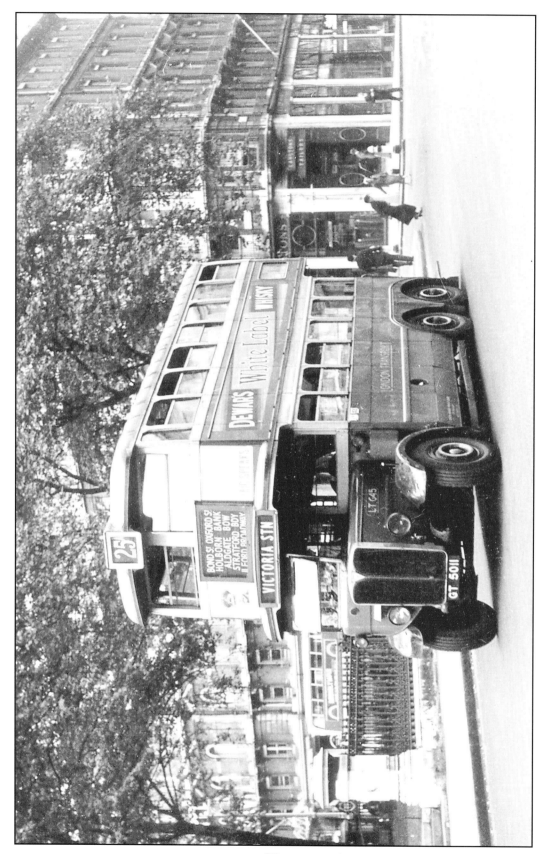

<<< *Opposite page:* **LT645** (**GT5011**) in Grosvenor Gardens in September 1934. This was the final style of Chiswick body for the 56-seat six-wheelers, after which the Bluebirds with increased seating capacity appeared.

This page: **STL1932** (**DLU283**) and **STL1883** (**DLU288**) represent the new generation of Chiswick products in service in September 1937 on Cricklewood garage's route 16. The route had recently lost its obsolete NS- and LS-class vehicles which had been full of character. They were only a decade older than the STLs but a world away in design. The LSs, too, had been none too reliable and the sight of one broken down by the kerb along the Edgware Road had become increasingly common as the nineteen-thirties advanced. In the STL can be recognised the Chiswick double-decker which became the Routemaster, still in service in 2000.

The Prewar STDs

The arrival of 100 Leyland-bodied Titan TD4s in 1937 caused no little stir in London bus circles. The bodywork had been superficially disguised as a Chiswick design but was very different in construction and was instantly recognisable. All 100 ran from Hendon garage, although some were later allocated elsewhere from time to time. They are perhaps best remembered on route 183 which ran from Golders Green to Northwood station at its furthest extent with many journeys terminating at Harrow or Pinner. **STD26 (DLU336)** *(above)* and **STD94 (DLU404)** were brand new in these Hendon views. STD94 was one of the last ten which had torque-converter transmission, soon replaced with crash (or "clash", as London Transport termed them) gearboxes. These immaculately turned out buses with drivers equally smart in white dustcoats and white-top uniform caps epitomise all that was best about London Transport before the war.

One of Geoffrey Atkins's most famous photographs. Station Road, West Hendon in 1937 was host to **STD64 (DLU374)**, a crash gearbox example, and one of the torque-converter vehicles with bonnet number between STD91 and STD 100. STD64 was on the 83A, a Sundays only route from Kew Green to Golders Green, and the other bus was on the 183. STD64's smartly turned out driver looks at the photographer whilst its conducter stands on the pavement as passengers board the bus.

London by Night

Geoffrey Atkins has produced many fine shots taken after dark, among the best of which are these two September 1954 views taken at the top of Whitehall. In the view above, taken according to Big Ben at 7.17pm, **RT1583 (KLB671)** is not long out of Victoria on a short working as far as Highgate. A fine Southampton-registered Vauxhall saloon car is poised to beat the RT away from the lights. In the view below **RTW178 (KLB908)** is on the famous route 11 bound for Liverpool Street. The affectionate young couple in the upstairs front seat were blissfully unaware that they were being immortalised on film. Although Geoffrey Atkins had little affection for the ex-independent Leyland Titans, one of them managed to creep into the magnificent view (>>> *following page*) of Piccadilly Circus looking towards Shaftesbury Avenue. The fleet number of the Dodson-bodied Upton Park TD is unfortunately indecipherable.

London buses were frequent visitors abroad. The most celebrated such adventure was the despatch of two RTs and an RTL to North America in 1952. **RT2775 (LYR826)**, **RT2776 (LYR827)** and **RTL1307 (LYR935)** were the vehicles chosen. The RTs had Park Royal bodies and the RTL a Weymann unit, the first of that make on this type of chassis. They are seen in this view at the Earl's Court Commercial Motor Show after their return to Great Britain, bearing various transatlantic fixtures and fittings. The Fordson Thames E83W 10-cwt service van which accompanied the buses is also in the picture. The van was fitted with a generator to provide lighting for the interior of the RTL during stops. The London bus stop had accompanied the buses on the tour.

Standard Type Variants in 1950

These two vehicles could scarcely, despite looking superficially alike, have been more different. Granted that the bodies were identical, there was little or no similarity between the chassis. **SRT54 (FJJ753)** was a rebodied prewar chassis, STL2653, which did not survive long in London Transport service. It had been taken into stock in May 1949 and was withdrawn in May 1954. **RTL14 (JXN334)**, on the other hand, was a postwar Leyland PD2 chassis adapted for the LTE. Delivered in December 1948, it was one of a successful variant which eventually totalled 1,631 and might have been expected to give more years of reliable service than it did. It was withdrawn in its prime and sold in January 1958.

Postwar Leylands on Route 76

Geoffrey Atkins was partial to route 76 views. Certainly at Victoria, one of the photographer's favourite spots, the 76 stand left buses well-placed for uncluttered shots. We have seen studies of STs *(page 16)* and STLs *(pages 18/19)* and here are the postwar Leylands in the period before full blind displays were reintroduced. **RTL327** (**KGU285**) was running as AR8 in August 1953 and **RTW137** (**KGK637**) as AR5 in July 1952. The running numbers - the garage code "AR" plus a service number - indicated the position of the bus in the route's traffic plan for the day. In London the word "route", often pronounced "rowt", always referred to the roads and locations served, whereas "service" meant the frequency.

Postwar Leylands Compared

In these views from July 1952 at Victoria and August 1956 at Golders Green the RTL and RTW types are compared as are the reduced blind displays with the later full displays. At Victoria **RTW84** (**KGK584**) was on the 76 alongside **RTL579** (**KGU87**) on the 29. The reduced blinds themselves varied in that the final destination was below the route number for the 76 and above on the 29 blind. In the Golders Green scene **RTL1443** (**NLE717**) and **RTL665** (**KXW15**) were on the 28 to Wandsworth. The full sets of blinds include five intermediate points served, only one of which - Kensington High Street - was common to both. A stranger might have been forgiven for assuming that the two buses were to follow different routes between Golders Green and Wandsworth.

Early RTs

The only RT which can be genuinely referred to as "prewar", and at that only just, was RT1, the prototype registered EYK396, which entered service in August 1939, although the chassis had run with an earlier body as fleet number ST1140 as early as July 1938. The remaining 150 "prewar" RTs were wartime buses, though far removed from the austerity such a description normally evokes. RT2 - 151 took to the road between January 1940 and February 1942.Their bodies were substantially different in construction from the postwar standard, though visually there was less difference. The curved lower line of the cab windows and the final destination above the intermediate points display rather than below were the most obvious identifying features. **RT140 (FXT315)**, sporting a full set of blinds for New Cross garage's route 163 allocation, was on the Embankment in May 1955. **RT26 (FXT201)** was in Chiswick High Road in September 1957 on driver-training duties, a fate which befell many of the type.

Roof-box RTs at Victoria

The position of the route number on London double-deckers was a design feature which found Chiswick curiously uncertain. In the Capital more so than in other cities a bus stop might be served by several routes, often so many that separate bus-stop posts had to be provided at some locations. Outside Charing Cross station in the rush hour, for example, might see a dozen or more buses lining up to pick up passengers. In these conditions the passenger had to be able to see the route number with a minimum of difficulty. Putting it in the roofline ought to have been the answer, but Chiswick's uncertainty led to it being tried as an integral part of the between-decks three-part display, a style which eventually became the standard for the Routemaster and beyond. The roof-box style is shown on Park Royal-bodied **RT219** (**HLW206**) *(above)* and **RT1398** (**KWW497**) with bodywork by Saunders. The pictures were taken at Victoria in August 1950 and May 1955.

The Craven RT

The route number was in the roof on the variant of the RT body built by Cravens Railway Wagon and Carriage Company Limited. Despite its title, Cravens was experienced in bus-building and when, in the late forties, London Transport needed more bodies than Park Royal and Weymann could supply, orders were placed with Saunders Engineering & Shipyard Limited as well as with Cravens. A Saunders example is illustrated at the foot of page 33. It differed little from standard; only the offside route indicator plate, set further back, gave the game away at first glance. The first of 120 Cravens RTs was delivered in September 1948 and the batch was shared between the Central and Country Areas. **RT1424 (JXC187)** *(above)* was in green livery in July 1952. It was at Eccleston Bridge working as a relief on Green Line route 704. **RT1476 (KGK735)**, in red livery, was a Victoria garage allocation on route 52 in May 1955. The Cravens were visually very different and had five side windows instead of four. They were early withdrawals, both our examples going in Summer 1956.

Roof-box RTs at Golders Green

The Cravens body differed in more ways than simply the extra windows. It was, in fact, a thinly disguised standard Cravens product. They were nonetheless often difficult to spot in a traffic jam at first glance because Cravens had used the standard Chiswick-designed cab, windscreen and front mudguards. A closer look at either the front or rear profiles soon revealed the identity. The differences and - despite everything - the curious similarity are well shown in Geoffrey Atkins's Golders Green views of Cravens **RT1458 (JXC221)** *(above)* and Park Royal **RT505 (HLX322)**. The pictures date from September 1954 and August 1956. The Craven RTs - RT1458 also went in mid 1956 - went on to serve many other operators, often for longer than in London.

Traffic Scenes in Whitehall

Perhaps the most telling point made by these July 1952 pictures of London's most famous thoroughfare is the remarkable lack of other traffic. Although hideous traffic jams had been a feature of London life since the days of horse-drawn buses, they were certainly less prevalent than they are today. Whitehall, though, might have been expected to be busier in Summer 1952; these views could have been taken during the Suez crisis four years later. Nearly all the buses are of the RT family - RT, RTL and RTW variants are all represented - but in the background of the upper view lurks a utility Daimler on route 88. The stars are **RTW284 (KXW384)** on the 11 and **RT1836 (KYY691)** on the 12.

The Roof-box Banished and Full Blind Displays

Chiswick eventually decided on the three-part integral destination-blind display. Even then there was some hesitation, for on the Routemaster the route number would be on the right rather than on the left. Even though the roof-box variant of the RT was peculiarly "London" and the favourite of many London Transport watchers, the design as exemplified by these two photographs perhaps takes the palm as *the* classic London bus. **RT919** (**JXN297**) *(above)*, in a July 1954 picture, was working as running number X1 (X garage was Middle Row, North Kensington) on the 15. It was at Aldgate, faced with a long haul to the Coach & Horses at Kew Green. **RTL653** (**KXW3**) also had a lengthy run ahead of it in August 1956. It was Stockwell garage's SW29 at Golders Green on the 2A, waiting to leave for West Norwood.

Standard RTs at Victoria

Above: A driver strides purposefully towards the door of the staff canteen, doubtless in much need of a cuppa on a hot July day in 1952. Several overalled men are drinking theirs outside in the sunshine. In the meantime, Willesden garage's **RT3549** (**MLL859**) bakes gently as it awaits passengers and crew for a route 52 run to Ladbroke Grove.

Below: On the same day, green-liveried **RT3123** (**KXW232**) from Dorking garage had arrived at nearby Eccleston Bridge as a relief on Green Line route 712. The lack of an offside route-number plate was understandable on this duty, but at that date the missing rear wheel-cover was most unusual.

The Green Line RT

The RTs used for the East London Green Line routes running into Aldgate Minories bus and coach station were possibly the most handsome of them all. For a start they were devoid of pasted paper advertisements, which vastly improved their looks. The green livery was further enhanced by the provision on the upper-deck panels of a cast "Green Line" motif. The G^{REEN LIN}E fleetname with LONDON TRANSPORT encased in the underlining was also very distinctive. These visual differences were all the concession there was to coach status, however, for inside they were standard buses. These July 1954 views are of **RT3227 (KYY956)** and **RT3241 (KYY970)** at Aldgate, respectively on the 721 to Brentwood and the 722 to Upminster.

Experimental Routemasters

The event of the 1950s was the Routemaster. The first appeared in 1954 but did not carry passengers in public service until 1956. Four prototypes preceded the production version which took to the streets from 1958. The first, **RM1 (SLT56)**, was bodied by London Transport at Chiswick and originally had a flat front. It ran thus for a short period before modifications produced the add-on radiator grille seen in the picture above, taken at Victoria garage in September 1958. The third and fourth prototypes had Leyland running units. The latter was fitted out as a Green Line coach with bodywork by Eastern Coach Works, the only Routemaster so bodied. **CRL4 (SLT59)**, on the same day, was caught at Eccleston Bridge while working the 704 to Tunbridge Wells.

Production Routemasters

The Routemaster was at one and the same time no break at all with tradition - engine at the front next to a half-cab; rear open platform - and a revolution. Fully automatic transmission, power steering and *really* efficient brakes were none of them new but few designs had packaged them so successfully in one bus. They were a delight to drive in an age when provincial operators were still inflicting clutches, manual gearboxes and unassisted steering on their stage carriage drivers. They had their teething troubles, like any new concept, but soon settled down to become part of the London scene. **RM79 (VLT79)** *(above)* at Theobalds Road in September 1960 had no front opening windows on the upper deck, a design feature that was soon superseded by quarter-drop windows as seen on **RM1334 (334CLT)** at Marble Arch in September 1963.

The Leyland Atlanteans -- Fifty Leyland Atlanteans were bodied by Park Royal contemporaneously with the lengthened Routemasters, though scarcely to Routemaster standards of either comfort or appearance. There was no little difficulty in making them work properly, too, and the sight of one (or more) broken down along the line of route became so common an occurrence as no longer to inspire comment. Tottenham garage had had them inflicted on it for the 76 at the time of these May 1967 views of **XA18** (**CUV18C**) and **XA26** (**CUV26C**) at Victoria garage and passing Westminster Abbey.

>>> *Opposite page:* An early Green Line AEC Regal of the T class at Eccleston Bridge in September 1937. New in April 1930, **T74c** (**GF533**) had 27-seat, rear-entrance, Chiswick-built coachwork. Less than a year after this photograph was taken the coach was withdrawn and sold.

Green Line specified front entrances for later AEC Regals. With both types in service at the same time drivers had to be skilled in firstly remembering which type they were driving and then placing the entrance alongside the bus stop to avoid confusing intending passengers. **T207 (GK5493)** was photographed by Geoffrey Atkins in 1931 in its original Green Line livery and condition *(see page 9)*; here is the same vehicle *(<<< opposite page)* in London Transport's version of the Green Line colour scheme. The coach was at Charing Cross in August 1937, a year or so before it was converted for service bus work in which form it lasted until 1950. The shot of **T217 (GN2002)** *(above)* at Eccleston Bridge in the same month is notable for the magnificent Daimler limousine and the humble London taxicab. **T402 (PL6470)** *(below)* had been an East Surrey Traction Company vehicle. Its first LPTB number had been T318. It was at Victoria Coach Station, in September 1937.

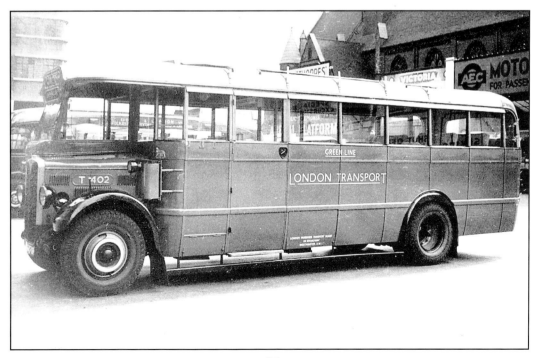

The AEC Q Type

These unusual vehicles, with their side-mounted vertical engines and entrance behind the front axle, were years ahead of their time and brought a touch of distinction to Green Line routes. **Q102c (CGJ207)**, bound for Ascot on route A1 in August 1937, was coincidentally followed onto Eccleston Bridge by **Q103c (CGJ208)** which was on the A2 to Sunningdale. Both routes had come into London from Gravesend and each coach had running number NF6. The Daimler limousine features again and an affectionate farewell is taking place among Q102c's intending passengers. This was perhaps the heyday of Green Line: comfortable, regular and frequent coaches by whose passing one might set the clock. The war and postwar traffic jams changed it all.

LPTB Green Line AEC Regals

The earlier T type coaches (see pages 45-47) were withdrawn from Green Line duties in 1938/39 and either sold or transferred to service bus duties, in the latter case converted or rebodied accordingly. Their replacements were a fine fleet of more modern AEC Regals in two series, known as 9T9 and 10T10 under Chiswick's chassis/body coding system. The 9T9s came in 1936, allowing various acquired coaches to be withdrawn. **T446c (CXX169)** at Eccleston Bridge in September 1937 represents these Weymann-bodied machines. A Vauxhall saloon has replaced the Daimler limousine. The celebrated 10T10s came two years later and swept away the LGOC-designed vehicles of the early thirties. In this case the bodies were built at Chiswick by London Transport. **T558 (ELP282)**, seen at Eccleston Bridge soon after entering service in June 1938 from Dorking garage, illustrates the detail frontal differences over the 9T9. The fared-in front wing arrangement presages that of the RT.

Underfloor-engined Leylands

Although Chiswick is often thought of as having been conservative, even somewhat hidebound, in matters of vehicle design, it had underfloor-engined coaches in successful front-line service before the war. The TF class was based on a Leyland chassis and a lot might have come of it much earlier had the war not intervened. There were two sorts of TF, a sightseeing coach with curved glass observation panels in the roof and a 34-seat Green Line coach, of which there were 75. In these two 1939 Aldgate views brand new **TF60c (FJJ671)** is contrasted with the conventional 10T10 type in the shape of **T703c** and **T682c (EYK338/317)**. TF60c and T682c were Romford garage allocations, T702c was working out of Grays.

Postwar Leyland Single deckers

When the war ended London Transport was in a difficult position. Its fleet had performed miracles during the war but had perforce been less than well maintained and had suffered much damage and loss through German bombing raids and blackout accidents. Ministry officials repaid this in the immediate aftermath of the war by liberal issue of stop notices on what they considered to be defective vehicles. The LPTB could not magic a purpose-built fleet out of thin air and was obliged to take into stock various off-the-peg designs. Thus the Leyland PS1 single-decker, in two versions to a total of 131, appeared as the London Transport TD class. **TD28** (**HGF986**) *(above)* and **TD65** (**JXC258**) represent the Weymann- and Mann Egerton-bodied versions. Both were Kingston garage allocations and the photographs were taken at Staines in May 1955.

Postwar Underfloor-engined Coaches

The postwar standard single-decker was the AEC Regal IV, a heavyweight design which served as long and as efficiently as its contemporary double-deck brethren of the RT family. As with the RT there were several variations on a theme. The first 25 units of the RF family were private hire coaches to dimensions of 27ft 6ins by 7ft 6ins, some of which were later converted for Green Line operation, exemplified by **RF19** (**LUC219**) *(above)* in a gloomy, wet Golders Green bus station in August 1956. Fifteen 30ft-long by 8ft-wide examples for similar duties followed. These Eastern Coach Works-bodied vehicles were less suited to conversion, having outward opening slam doors and no destination screens. **RFW5** (**LUC380**) was at Victoria Coach Station in September 1957. **RFW10** was behind and the pair were operating a Windsor and Hampton Court tour.

Standard RFs

Above: The version which most readily comes to mind when the RF family is considered is the 39-seat Green Line coach. Unlike the contemporary RT "coaches" *(see page 39)*, the RFs had deeper and more comfortable seats, luggage racks and air operated folding doors. **RF163 (MLL550)**, which had been new in February 1952, was at Eccleston Bridge the following July.

Below: The Country Area service bus version of the RF had 41 seats, no luggage racks and a slightly different livery. Examples were frequently seen standing in on Green Line routes, as was East Grinstead garage's **RF670** (**NLE670**) at Eccleston Bridge on route 708 in September 1956.

Further RF Variations

The Central Area version of the RF differed - apart from the red livery - in not having doors to the passenger entrance. The Metropolitan Police, which had control of such matters in London Transport's Central Area, had a history of extreme conservatism over such perfectly ordinary items as covered tops on double-deckers, driving-cab windscreens, pneumatic tyres and - in this case - doors, which it would not sanction. Such nonsenses eventually went their deserved way to oblivion, but in the 1950s passengers shivered. Red **RF326 (MLL963)** *(above)* was at Golders Green on route 210 for Finsbury Park in July 1954. In the mid 1960s 175 RFs were fitted with twin headlamps and given a restyled livery, as seen on **RF103 (LYF454)** at Victoria garage in May 1967. With a chassis similar to that of the RFW, the 65 1½-deck coaches owned by British European Airways were used for airport transfer duties. They were operated and maintained by London Transport although no fleet numbers were allocated. **MLL755** *(>>> opposite page)* was at Waterloo in May 1955.

<<< *Opposite page:* A London Transport disaster story. The 1965 RC class of 14 Willowbrook-bodied AEC Reliances, in an insipid mainly grey livery, were troublesome from the start and lasted little more than five years. **RC14 (CUV72C)** was on the 705 from Sevenoaks to Windsor, an express route which ran via Heathrow Airport and whose reliability was torn to shreds by the RCs allocated to it from Dunton Green and Windsor garages.

This page: Geoffrey Atkins did not ignore the London trolleybus fleet and in these two pictures recorded the earliest and latest series. Number **33 (MG185)** was at Kingston in September 1937 and Q1 **1868 (LYH868)** was in Chiswick High Road exactly 20 years later. Number 33 was a 56-seat AEC with Union Construction Co. bodywork; the Q was a BUT with 8ft-wide 70-seat bodywork by MCCW.

Standard Trolleybuses

Above: The first Class C1 vehicle, **132 (CGF132)**, was also the first of the hundreds of standard 70-seat London trolleybuses. It was a Weymann-bodied AEC, seen loading at Kew in August 1936.

Below: Trolleybus **200 (CUL200)** was a Class C2 machine, similar to the C1 apart from having MCCW bodywork instead of Weymann. In this August 1936 view at Hammersmith it was awaiting its departure time on route 667 for Hampton Court. These machines were very handsome and their appearance was enhanced by the streamlined rear wings.

Trolleybuses in the 1950s

Above: The C2s were still among the most handsome of all London trolleybuses in the postwar period. This one, **216 (CUL216)**, was spotted at Edgware in September 1954 as the photographer was passing by on his way into London and the photograph was too good to miss. The trolleybus was on service 664 to Paddington via Cricklewood and Harlesden. *Below:* In the same month, a typical scene at Aldgate Minories, with trolleybuses and a Green Line RF. By simply turning through 360 degrees the photographer could also capture Green Line RTs and Central Area RTs and RTLs. The trolleybuses are **1568 (FXH568)**, a BRCW-bodied AEC of Class N1, and **1649 (FXH649)**, an N2 with similar AEC chassis and Park Royal body. The heavier front dome and pillar treatment on the N2 was an identifying feature.

The Four Faces of London Transport

The highbridge double-decker *was* the London bus in the fifties and early sixties. The writer was aware of this in a quite indefinable way. The single-deckers were at the same time part of the general scheme of things, yet stood apart. Attempts to explain to non-enthusiasts the fascination which London Transport inspired were usually doomed to failure. *"Yes, but they are all the same. Well ... There's the Green Line, of course, they're different. And then there's the little bus to Edgware or the Spaniards."* The "little" bus was either a TD or an RF and the tenor of such conversations suggested that even to the non-enthusiast the double-decker was a normal London bus, whereas the others had to be categorised in some way.

In this quartet of views Geoffrey Atkins recorded the detail one saw as the bus (or trolleybus) glided into the stop. In the case of the RT family the route number and destination had already been spotted as the bus approached and one then looked for the information board above the bonnet. If it was not there, the bus was not properly dressed. In later years, as standards dropped, they were frequently absent. The Routemaster had a similar arrangement, but above the lower-saloon window, which usually - at least in the early years of the type - announced that "This is the new Routemaster". The principal visual difference, apart from the radiator, between the RT and the RTL lay in the dumb irons. The cab-front body panel for the RT would at first not clear these more cumbersome Leyland dumb irons. Its design was revised, as seen in these views, to incorporate an upward curve allowing all standard postwar bodies to fit all chassis.

This page: In scenes three and a half decades apart trolleybus activity is compared with motorbus operations. At Kew in the sunshine of August 1936 *(above)* three route 667 trolleybuses and one 657 are catering to the crowds flocking to Kew Gardens and Hampton Court. The RT was far from dead in 1970: Victoria garage in March *(below)* had **RT3363** (**LYR582**) on front line route 10 duties, surrounded by Routemasters.

>>> *Opposite page:* From London Transport's inception in 1933 there had never been a new vehicle so dramatically different from that which had gone before as the Strachan-bodied AEC Merlin of 1966, introduced for an equally revolutionary type of short-haul West End route, known as Red Arrow. **XMS5** (**JLA55D**), in service since April 1966, was at Victoria the following September. Cricklewood garage's **RM1375** (**375CLT**) stands alongside on route 16.

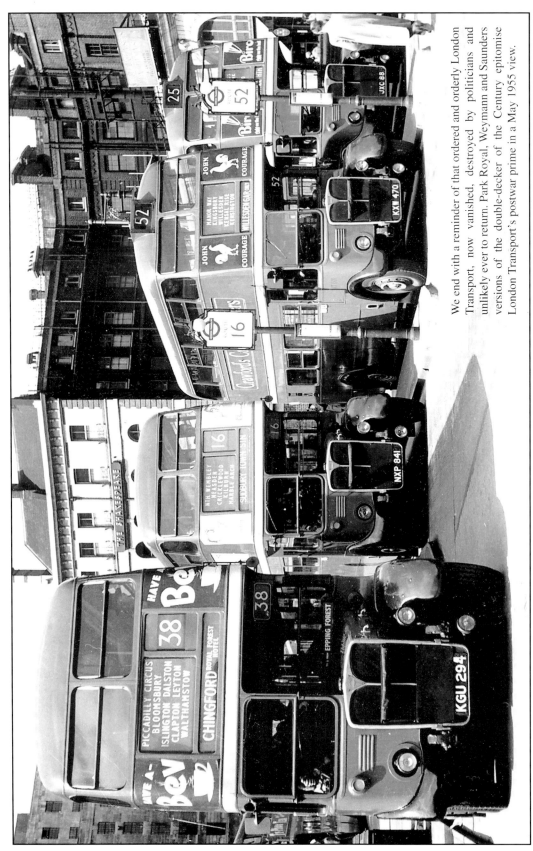

We end with a reminder of that ordered and orderly London Transport, now vanished, destroyed by politicians and unlikely ever to return. Park Royal, Weymann and Saunders versions of the double-decker of the Century epitomise London Transport's postwar prime in a May 1955 view.